D1614341

Early Years

Over a thousand years ago, the tribes of the **Iroquois** pushed into the forests of what is now New York State. They settled in large dwellings called **longhouses** in this land of streams and lakes between the Adirondack Mountains and Niagara Falls. Many Native American tribes spoke **Iroquoian** languages, but only five northeastern tribes—the Cayuga, Mohawk, Oneida, Onondaga, and Seneca—united into a powerful group known as the Iroquois **Confederacy** or the League of the Iroquois. The name *Iroquois* (pronounced EAR-ah-koy in the United States and EAR-ah-kwah in Canada) is a French version of **Irinakhoiw**, meaning "poisonous snakes." The name was given to these tribes by their enemy, the Ojibwe, who lived in the area of the Great Lakes. The Iroquois called themselves **Haudenosaunee**, an Iroquoian word, meaning "People of the Longhouse."

The people of the longhouse gradually expanded their territory around the lower Great Lakes of Huron, Ontario, and Erie, along with Lake Champlain and Lake George. They also

Around the village the Iroquois built a tall log fence called a **palisade**. The palisade was made of sharpened logs set into the ground and lashed together. Lining the inside walls were platforms where lookouts warned villagers of enemy attack. The Iroquois even made the entrance into a maze to confuse and slow attackers.

Within the palisade, they built several large dwellings called longhouses. Small communities might have just a few, while large villages had 30 to 150 longhouses. Every village also had sweat lodges, storage buildings, racks for drying and stretching animal hides, and pits called middens for burying garbage.

In fields near the village, Iroquois women grew crops of corn, beans, and squash. They also gathered berries, nuts, and fruit in the forests around them. While the children played and did chores, they worked together to provide food and make clothing for their families. Women tended to stay near the village while men trotted along paths among the trees and paddled canoes on the many rivers. They traveled widely through their territory to hunt game, trade with their friends, and fight against their enemies.

These steps lead to the platforms inside the palisade walls where the Iroquois watched for the approach of enemy attackers.

Several families lived in each longhouse, which provided shelter from both summer heat and winter cold.

Men remained clan members for life. They waged war, fished, and hunted together.

Clans

Iroquois life centered on clans whose members were related to a common ancestor. There were ten clans: Turtle, Bear, Wolf, Beaver, Deer, Hawk, Ball, Heron, Snipe, and Eel. Clan members lived together, sharing food and fire in the longhouse. The men in the clan hunted together while the women and children worked together in the fields.

The clan also chose its own leaders, who served on a village council. This council dealt with hunting, fishing, farming, and religious ceremonies. The tribe itself was made up of all the villages. It was represented by a council of chiefs from each of the clans. The tribal council discussed warfare and other serious matters that affected all the groups. Everyone on the council discussed a problem until there was consensus, or general agreement.

Women did not take part in councils, but they still had great influence. They headed the households and everything inside the longhouse belonged to the women—even the longhouse itself. Men owned only their clothes, tools, and

weapons. Children were born into their mother's clan. When a man got married he moved into his wife's longhouse. He remained a member of his old clan, but his children were members of their mother's clan.

A group of family members called the **ohwachira** managed the longhouse. The oldest woman, known as the **clan mother**, served as the leader. She oversaw all the work of the women and settled arguments in the longhouse. She gathered people for seasonal rituals. Most importantly, she chose the man who represented the clan on the village council. She then advised him and made sure he followed the laws that bound the people together.

Iroquois women managed their households and owned most of the property within each longhouse.

planted sunflowe
for many dishes.
used in ceremon
In early summ
other greens. Th
early berries and
corn ripening on

Iroquois Confederacy

For many years the Iroquois tribes fought among themselves. However, the five tribes finally declared a truce and formed the **Iroquois Confederacy,** or the League of the Iroquois, around 1570. It is believed that a Huron leader named **Deganawidah,** along with a Mohawk chief named **Hiawatha,**

Making Meals

The Iroquois stored much of the autumn harvest so they'd have enough food for the winter. Women cut meat into strips which they slowly dried over a fire. They pounded corn kernels into meal, which was then roasted to make **parched corn**. Parched corn was placed in bark barrels and stored in pits in the ground, along with squash, dried meat, and other foods.

Women prepared meals over longhouse fires—roasting or boiling fish and wild game. They often flavored soups and stews with dried nuts or berries. However, corn was their most important food. They grew several kinds, which they used in soups, stews, puddings, and bread. Green ears of corn were boiled or roasted; sometimes kernels were scraped from the cob and fried in bread or used in soups. Corn soup was a favorite dish, as was **succotash**, a mixture of corn, beans, and hominy. To make hominy, women boiled corn with wood ashes to loosen the hulls. Sometimes they ground corn with a mortar and pestle and then mixed the cornmeal with maple sugar, dried berries, or chopped dried meat.

Ground cornmeal was often stored in baskets until it was used to make bread or was added to soups and stews.